INSTRUCTORS GUIDE

THE PART-TIMER PRIMER™

A Teen's Guide to Surviving the Hiring Process and Landing Your First Job

Darrell Doepke

FIRST EDITION   Copyright 2013   Darrell Doepke

1

TABLE OF CONTENTS

Introduction for Instructors

Hello instructors. Whether you are a teacher, counselor, coach or any other role you might fill as a mentor, the task of teaching life and career skills to young adults seems to fall more and more on your shoulders. Thank you for taking an interest in this subject. As you already know, there is great satisfaction in watching your willing students absorb the information you provide them, bloom and grow from it, and take another step closer to mature and responsible adulthood.

In this Instructors Guide I have created lesson plans and quizzes for you, complete with answer guides and discussion points. Although my suggestion is to break the subject matter into six classes or sections, you'll have a better feel with your own students as to how best to offer up the information.

Thank you for helping them prepare to take that first scary leap into the working world!

Lesson Plan for Day 1: "Introduction"

Agenda:
- Demo Album and Album One: Pages 1-32

Time Commitment:
- Second half of class period

Details:
You will be introducing your students to the book for the first time. When they read these first two albums, they will learn about the realities that teens with no work experience must face. In the next class you'll discuss how and why first-timers often fall short of the decision maker's expectations. You'll tell them in great detail what to expect during the application stage– and how to prepare for it. For today, they need to understand that there is a process of elimination that happens long before they'll ever get to a face-to-face interview with an employer. That's what the book is all about-- preparing them for the hiring process.

Goals:
- Introduce the students to the topic.

- Let them know that you are going to help them understand and prepare for the hiring process, including everything that happens before the interview stage.

- Assure them that their chances of finding their first job will greatly improve if they know how to prepare for the hiring process.

Question and Answer Session:
Prompt the discussion with questions like these, and see where their answers take you:

- "How many of you have ever had a job before? Not a babysitting or lawn mowing or pet walking job; a job where a company hired you, put you to work at their place of business, and gave you a paycheck?"

- "If you have a job, or had a job, how did you get it? What did you have to do? Who did you have to talk to? Why do you think you got the job?"

- "If you've never had a job before, what would you have to do to get one? What steps would you have to take?"

- "What kinds of jobs are out there for people like you who have never had a job before?"

- "What kinds of skills do you think you would need in order to get a job like that?"

- "If you see a help-wanted ad and you apply for a job, how many other people do you think will be applying for that same job?"

- "If 50 other people apply for the same job, how are you going to convince the company they should hire you when you have no job experience? No work history?"

- "How many of you know what to expect during a job interview? Do you know what questions they will ask you? What information are they looking for about you?"

- "What if I told you that the vast majority of people who apply for a job never get a job interview? They never get that far in the process. Why do you think that is?"

- "Did you know that there is a weeding-out process that happens long before most people ever get to meet with an interviewer? Why would that be?"

- "If you are not even aware of this weeding-out process, how would you know how to prepare for it? How fair is that?"

- "What do you feel is the scariest part about going out and getting a job?"

- "If you knew ahead of time what the hiring process was all about; knew what the decision makers are looking for in a new hire; knew how to <u>get to</u> the interview stage; knew how to study and prepare for the questions they will ask you; how confident would that make you feel about finding a job?"

Homework Assignment:
"Read pages 1-32 and be prepared to discuss the information in the next class." That sounds like a lot of reading, but the entire book can be read in two hours or less. It should take them 30-45 minutes to read these pages.

Evaluation:
When this class meets again, you will hand out a quiz after you have reviewed and discussed the homework material.

Lesson Plan for Day 2: "Prepare for the Process"

Agenda:
- Review previous day's homework assignment
- Quiz 1
- Answers to Quiz 1
- The Job Application Form

Time Commitment:
- One full class period

Details:
You will ask for and answer any questions from the previous day's homework assignment, then hand out Quiz 1. After your students turn in the completed quizzes, discuss each question and give them the answers if time allows. Before class ends, you will hand out a blank job application form and ask them to take it home, fill it out and bring it back when this class meets again.

Goals:
- Review the correct answers to Quiz 1.
- Introduce them to the Job Application Form and the process of filling one out.

Review Prior to Quiz 1:
Ask for questions, and prompt the discussion with these:

- Before you can get a job, you need to get what? (*Get an interview.*)

- Is an actual face-to-face job interview one of the <u>first</u> steps, or one of the last steps of the hiring process? (*Last.*)

- What are the first steps of the hiring process before you get to the face-to-face interview? (*Filling out a job app properly; completing a survey.*)

- Do employers typically read through every single job app completely and thoroughly? (*No; they don't have time.*)

- What are some of the ways that employers try to "weed you out" before you can get to the interview stage? (*Checking your spelling and grammar; checking to see if you filled out the job app completely; checking social media sites for inappropriate language or behavior.*)

- What is one way to try and stand out from everyone else who is applying for the same job? (*Find something that is <u>different</u> about you, whether you think it is relevant or not.*)

- What are some of examples of being different in a way that might be meaningful, or might get the attention of the employer? (*Aspiring to a certain career or profession; playing an instrument; being on a team; earning an award or certification; caring for a pet; volunteering; there are lots of ways.*)

- Can you know for sure if you have something that is meaningfully different? (*No, you can't. You're just trying and hoping that something you write down here will catch the attention of the employer in a positive way.*)

Hand Out Quiz 1: Questions from Demo Album and Album 1
Collect quizzes for review/grading. Review answers as time allows.

Homework Assignment:

Hand each student a blank job application form (included in this Instructors Guide on pages 12-13); have them take it home tonight and fill it out as if they were applying for a real job.

Prompt the discussion about tonight's homework assignment with questions like these:

- "When you take this job application home tonight and fill it out, remember what you read about yesterday. What are the first things an employer is going to look for?" (*Spelling and grammar.*)
- "If you are having trouble filling out a particular section, what should you do?" (*Ask someone to help you.*)
- "If a certain section of the job app form does not apply to you, should you just leave it blank? (*No.*) What should you do in that section?" (*Write N/A for Not Applicable.*)
- "What is one of the most important sections of the job app form, especially for someone with no job experience?" (*The "General Information" section.*)
- "Why is the General Information section so important to first-time job hunters?" (*It gives them a chance to explain how they are different. And different is memorable.*)

Evaluation:

Next class you will collect the completed job application forms, then hand out and/or display an example of a properly completed form (included in this Instructors Guide on pages 22-23) for review, comparison and discussion.

Circle the <u>one</u> answer you think is correct for each question. For questions that require you to write in the answer, please write neatly and clearly; unreadable answers will be considered incorrect.

<u>**1.**</u> When the former United States President Abraham Lincoln said, "*Give me six hours to chop down a tree, and I will spend the first four sharpening the axe,*" the point he was making was that:

    a) tools weren't very sharp back in the 1800's.

    b) the key to any successful activity is preparation.

    c) it takes longer than you think to chop down a tree with an axe.

<u>**2.**</u> Before you can get a job, you need to get a job *interview*. But before you can get an interview, you need to:

    a) convince the business owner or decision maker that you are
         worth the chance.

    b) survive a weeding-out process that happens long before you
         ever get to an interview.

    c) understand how to fill out a job application.

    d) all of the above.

<u>**3.**</u> When it comes to hiring new employees, the small business owner needs to _____ the process as much as possible.

    a) draw out

    b) streamline

    c) complicate

    d) slow down

<u>**4.**</u> If a business owner ends up hiring the "wrong person" and has to let them go, the owner has now wasted both _____ and _____.

5. When are the worst times to just "drop in" to see the owner or manager?

    a) when the business first opens.

    b) when the owner is eating lunch.

    c) when the store is very busy.

    d) all of the above.

6. A small business owner usually reads through every job application completely and thoroughly.

    True   False

7. Correct spelling and grammar are very important in leaving a good first impression.

    True   False

8. When would it be appropriate for a parent to stop in and pick up a job application?

    a) When the parent is looking for a job for themselves.

    b) When their child is too busy with sports after school.

    c) When their child doesn't feel like stopping in and getting one.

9. It is OK to leave a job application completely blank and just staple your resume to it. It saves you a lot of time.

    True   False

10. What might be one of the first things that a business owner checks when reviewing a job application?

    a) your eye color

    b) your spelling and grammar

    c) your previous work experience

11. Why is it important to fill out a job application completely and carefully?

   a) It shows that you are willing and able to follow instructions.

   b) It shows that you pay attention to details.

   c) Other people won't fill it out completely, which will give you an edge in getting to the interview stage.

   d) All of the above.

12. When filling out an online survey, answer all the questions honestly and don't try to "fake out" the survey.

   True   False

13. Why are employers interested in what they can find out about you on Facebook, MySpace and other social media sites?

   a) They want to stay current on social media trends.

   b) They want to be your friend.

   c) They assume that you will be on your best behavior during a job interview, so they are looking for clues that might show them the type of person you *really* are.

14. Getting noticed for a job is not so much a matter of being "better" than someone else. Quite often it is a matter of being "different" in ways that are meaningful to a potential employer (whether you realize it or not). List at least <u>one</u> thing about yourself that might make you stand out from other people applying for the same job.

_____

_____

_____

Homework Assignment

"You will be given an actual job application form. Please fill out this form completely, carefully, and to the best of your ability. The position you are applying for is **Crew Member**. If a certain question or section does not apply to you, fill it in with **N/A** which means "Not Applicable." All job applications will be reviewed by your instructor, and might also be reviewed by fellow students in a class exercise. **Do not fill in your name on the application; it has already been filled in for you.**"

APPLICATION FOR EMPLOYMENT

Your response to any question will not be used as a basis for discrimination, but will be judged on its relevance to the position you are seeking. Wolfe It Down, Inc., a franchisee of XXXXXXXXXXX, is an equal opportunity employer.

Please complete the entire application to ensure processing.

PERSONAL INFORMATION (Please print)

Date: ____ / ____ / _____

Name (Last)	First	Middle	Do you have a Social Security Number?
EMPLOYEE	POTENTIAL	NEW	____ Yes ____ No

Are you less than 18 years of age? ____ Yes ____ No   (We are required to comply with federal and state laws concerning the employment of minors.)

Present Address _____ City _____ State _____ ZIP Code

Phone Number: _____ Email Address: _____ How were you referred to this company?

EMPLOYMENT DESIRED

(Please keep in mind that the availability of hours may vary.)

Position: _____   Date You Can Start: _____

	Mon 8am-8pm	Tue 8am-8pm	Wed 8am-8pm	Thu 8am-8pm	Fri 8am-9pm	Sat 8am-9pm	Sun 8am-8pm
We are open seven days a week:							
What hours would you be available to work for each day of the week?							

Are you able to work overtime? ____ Yes ____ No

Have you worked for our company before? _____ If Yes: where and when? _____

LEGAL

(All new hires will be required to provide proof of eligibility to work in the U.S.)

Are you legally eligible to work in the U.S.? ____ Yes ____ No

Have you been convicted of a crime in the last seven years or are currently under felony indictment? ____ Yes ____ No

If Yes, list convictions or indictments that are a matter of public record (arrests are not convictions). This will not necessarily disqualify you for employment.

Convictions/ Indictments: _____

Was your employment ever terminated by any of your previous employers? ____ Yes ____ No ____ N/A

If Yes, please give the name of the company or companies, and describe the reason(s) why your employment was terminated: _____

U.S. MILITARY SERVICE

Branch of Service   Technical Specialization   Rank Attained

EDUCATION

	Name and Location of School	Did you graduate?	Last Year Completed	Degree/ Area of Study
High School		Y N	1 2 3 4	
College		Y N	1 2 3 4	
Trade School		Y N	1 2 3 4	
Other		Y N	1 2 3 4	

GENERAL INFORMATION

List any skills, training, hobbies, classes, subjects of special interest, etc.

What special tools or equipment can you operate? _____ Can you operate a computer? ____ Yes ____ No

If Yes, what programs? _____

FORMER EMPLOYERS

List your last three employers, starting with the most recent one first.
Please complete this section even if you attach a resume.

Date (M/D/Y)	Name and Address of Employer	Wages	Position(s) Held
From: To:		Starting:_____ Ending:_____ If hourly, average number of hours per week: _____	

What was your reason for leaving: _____

Date (M/D/Y)	Name and Address of Employer	Wages	Position(s) Held
From: To:		Starting:_____ Ending:_____ If hourly, average number of hours per week: _____	

What was your reason for leaving: _____

Date (M/D/Y)	Name and Address of Employer	Wages	Position(s) Held
From: To:		Starting:_____ Ending:_____ If hourly, average number of hours per week: _____	

What was your reason for leaving: _____

PLEASE READ CAREFULLY

I HEREBY AUTHORIZE Wolfe It Down, Inc. to thoroughly investigate my background, references, employment record and other matters related to my suitability for employment. I authorize persons, schools, my current employer (if applicable), and previous employers and organizations contacted by Wolfe It Down, Inc. to provide any relevant information regarding my current and/or previous employment and I release all persons, schools, employers of any and all claims for providing such information. I understand that misrepresentation or omission of facts may result in rejection of this application, or if hired, discipline up to and including dismissal. I understand that nothing contained in this application, or conveyed during any interview which may be granted, is intended to create an employment contract. I understand that filling out this form does not indicate that there is a position open and does not obligate Wolfe It Down, Inc. to hire me. I understand and agree that my employment is at will, which means that it is for no specified period and may be terminated by me or by Wolfe It Down, Inc. at any time without prior notice for any reason.

Signature _____ Date _____

WOLFE IT DOWN, INC.
a Franchisee of XXXXXXXXXXXXXXXXX
XXXX W. Union Hills Drive, Suite 101
XXXXXXX, XX XXXXX

WE ARE AN EQUAL OPPORTUNITY EMPLOYER
COMMITTED TO HIRING A DIVERSE WORKFORCE.

Answer Guide and Page References

Question 1: When the former United States President Abraham Lincoln said, "*Give me six hours to chop down a tree, and I will spend the first four sharpening the axe,*" the point he was making was that:

   a) tools weren't very sharp back in the 1800's.

   b) the key to any successful activity is preparation.

   c) it takes longer than you think to chop down a tree with an axe.

Answer: b) <u>the key to any successful activity is preparation</u>.

Discussion (page 8): Abraham Lincoln clearly understood the importance of preparation. Any task or skill that is made to look easy has many hours of practice and preparation behind it. Think about the basketball player who makes 90% of his or her free throws; the finger-picking guitar player who doesn't miss a note and makes it look effortless; the singer who hits the high notes with ease. Those who are prepared have the best chance of succeeding.

Question 2: Before you can get a job, you need to get a job *interview*. But before you can get an interview, you need to:

   a) convince the business owner or decision maker that you are
       worth the chance.

   b) survive a weeding-out process that happens long before you
       ever get to an interview.

   c) understand how to fill out a job application.

   d) all of the above.

Answer: d) <u>all of the above</u>.

Discussion (page 10-11): The majority of people applying for a particular job never get to the actual job interview stage of the process. They were weeded out long before that, and most of the time they never find out why. The people in charge of hiring are going to use a variety of screening techniques to narrow their search down to a manageable number; they don't have time to meet with every single job applicant. For the teenager who has never had a job before, it is a steep uphill climb to convince someone that they should take a chance and hire you. Knowing how to properly fill out a job app can give them an edge over their "competitors" vying for the same job.

Question 3: When it comes to hiring new employees, the small business owner needs to _____ the process as much as possible.

a) draw out

b) streamline

c) complicate

d) slow down

Answer: b) streamline

Discussion (page 15): Streamlining the hiring process is a necessity. Remember all of the "hats" that were described on page 15? The business owner or hiring manager is already extremely busy with multiple tasks every day. So they will look for ways to make every task, including the hiring process, as efficient as possible so they don't waste their time.

Question 4: If a business owner ends up hiring the "wrong person" and has to let them go, the owner has now wasted both _____ and _____.

Answer: time and money

Discussion (page 17): The process of hiring and training a new employee takes up a lot of time. And while they are being trained, they are "on the clock" and being paid for their time. Keep in mind that all of this is over and above the normal time and expense of running a business. So if a new hire only lasts a week or two, then that time and money has been wasted.

Question 5: When are the worst times to just "drop in" to see the owner or manager?

a) when the business first opens.

b) when the owner is eating lunch.

c) when the store is very busy.

d) all of the above.

Answer: d) all of the above

Discussion (page 18): When a business opens its doors to the public at the beginning of the business day, often there is an initial "rush" of activity. Even before the doors open, there is often "prep work" being done that isn't quite finished yet. Stopping in at this time is not a good idea. In the foodservice industry, for example, restaurants are busiest during the typical breakfast, lunch and dinner hours, so definitely avoid those times. And you never know when the owner or manager might be on break. The bottom line is: stopping in unannounced is risky. If you're going to do it, take an approach such as this: "Hi, I stopped in to see about job opportunities here. Is this a good time to speak with someone, or is there a better time?" You might get a "let me see if she's available right now; hang on a minute," or perhaps a "best time to call is between ____ and ____" or "all of our applications are done online."

Question 6: A small business owner usually reads through every job application completely and thoroughly.

    True   False

Answer: <u>False</u>

Discussion (page 19): Remember that a job posting can generate dozens, even hundreds of job applications. There is not enough time in the day for anyone to read through each application entirely. The decision maker will quickly skim through the stack of job apps, looking for ways to eliminate people from contention and reduce the pile to a more manageable number. This is the beginning of the weeding-out process.

Question 7: Correct spelling and grammar are very important in leaving a good first impression.

    True   False

Answer: <u>True</u>

Discussion (page 20): Someone who uses correct spelling and grammar is perceived to be smart and detail-oriented. That perception leaves a positive first impression with decision makers.

Question 8: When would it be appropriate for a parent to stop in and pick up a job application?

    a) When the parent is looking for a job for themselves.

    b) When their child is too busy with sports after school.

    c) When their child doesn't feel like stopping in and getting one.

Answer: a) <u>When the parent is looking for a job for themselves.</u>

Discussion (page 23): The decision maker needs to see that you have enough interest and initiative to apply for a job on your own. It's not your parent's responsibility to find a job for you.

Question 9: It is OK to leave a job application completely blank and just staple your resume to it. It saves you a lot of time.

    True   False

Answer: <u>False</u>

Discussion (page 24): A business owner or manager is looking to see if you can follow instructions. If you can't follow instructions, then you won't be a good employee. Stapling a resume to a blank job app can also make you look lazy. That won't get you the job, either.

Question 10: What might be one of the first things that a business owner checks when reviewing a job application?

    a) your eye color

    b) your spelling and grammar

    c) your previous work experience

Answer: b) <u>your spelling and grammar</u>

Discussion (Page 25): To many employers, poor spelling, grammar and handwriting means sloppy work, and that won't get you hired.

Question 11: Why is it important to fill out a job application completely and carefully?

    a) It shows that you are willing and able to follow instructions.

    b) It shows that you pay attention to details.

    c) Other people won't fill it out completely, which will give you an edge in getting to the interview stage.

    d) All of the above.

Answer: d) <u>all of the above</u>

Discussion (page 24): Too many first-timers eliminate themselves from contention right off the bat by failing this most basic requirement. They make it easy for the owner or manager to toss their job app into the "No" pile. Finding that first job can be a long, slow, tedious process. It almost becomes a "battle of attrition" or "survival of the fittest," and it all starts with the job app.

Question 12: When filling out an online survey, answer all the questions honestly and don't try to "fake out" the survey.

   True   False

Answer: True

Discussion (page 30): Whether a business is trying to figure out how honest you are, how motivated you are, or how well you get along with others, there will be several different questions that all relate to the same issue. If you try to answer the questions by "telling them what they want to hear," you might actually trip yourself up.

Question 13: Why are employers interested in what they can find out about you on Facebook, MySpace and other social media sites?

   a) They want to stay current on social media trends.

   b) They want to be your friend.

   c) They assume that you will be on your best behavior during a job interview, so they are looking for clues that might show them the type of person you *really* are.

Answer: c) They assume that you will be on your best behavior during a job interview, so they are looking for clues that might show them the type of person you *really* are.

Discussion (page 32): The content that you post on social media is probably going to be a more accurate glimpse of "the real you." For many young adults, it's easy to adapt your personality to a situation such as a job interview; you can be on your best behavior when you want to be. And employers know that.

Question 14: Getting noticed for a job is not so much a matter of being "better" than someone else. Quite often it is a matter of being "different" in ways that are meaningful to a potential employer (whether you realize it or not). List at least <u>one</u> thing about yourself that might make you stand out from other people applying for the same job.

Answer: Each answer will be different.

Discussion (page 26-27): Previous work experience is obviously not a factor if someone has never had a job before. Encourage your students to think about what school subjects they seem to do well in; what hobbies or activities they are interested in outside of school; what particular skills they may have. Refer to the examples I listed on page 27. Try to identify <u>something</u> that might make each student unique in their own way. If you can't find one, they might need your help to develop one. They'll need to understand how "different" can be relevant and meaningful to a potential employer. This is not an easy task, but it is so important. This exercise can aid in improving a student's self-

worth and self-esteem, but also be on the lookout for a student who might feel dejected or embarrassed if they don't feel there is anything "worthy" about themselves.

Homework Assignment

After you collect the quizzes, you will hand each student an actual job application form. Ask them to take it home and fill it out completely, carefully, and to the best of their ability. The position they are applying for is **Crew Member**. If a certain question or section does not apply to them, they should fill it in with **N/A** which means "Not Applicable." All job applications will be reviewed by you, and might also be reviewed by fellow students in a class exercise.

They should not fill in their name on the application. Without their names on the application, it will be easier to discuss areas for improvement in a group setting.

Lesson Plan for Day 3: "The Job Application Form"

Agenda:
- Quiz 1 results
- Properly completed job application form

Time Commitment:
- One full class period

Details:
During the first half of the class, you will review the correct answers to Quiz 1. During the second half of class, you will review with your students a properly completed job application form. Tonight you will grade them on how well they filled it out.

Goals:
- Hand out results from Quiz 1. Review any questions that students seemed to get wrong the most.

- Collect completed job apps from students. (With colored markers, highlight the areas where they did well and where they could still use some improvement.)

- Copy and hand out sample of a properly completed job app and walk them through each section. Show how it is filled out completely with good spelling and grammar. Have them keep it as a sample of how to fill one out properly.

Homework Assignment:
"Read pages 33-43 and be prepared to discuss the information in the next class."

Tell your students that you're assuming they have all made it through these first weeding-out stages of the hiring process. But now the hurdles get higher. Employers need more information before they invest much time in them. Tonight's reading assignment will deal with email and phone screening techniques that aim to ferret out more weak candidates and reduce the chances of an employer wasting time talking to someone who is not going to be a good fit for the business. Your students will learn how to survive these screens and advance closer to the face-to-face interview.

Evaluation:
Using colored markers on the completed job apps, highlight the areas where they did well and where they could still use some improvement. Hand them back in the next class period.

Discussion: The written job application on pages 22-23 has been filled out completely and carefully, with correct spelling, grammar and handwriting that is neat and readable. Use this as an example of how a completed job app should look. During class discussion, you might hand out or display actual examples of how some of your students filled them out. Without their names on the application, it will be easier to discuss areas for improvement in a group setting. The point of the group exercise is not to identify specific individuals who need help; you can do that in one-on-one meetings with each student.

APPLICATION FOR EMPLOYMENT

Your response to any question will not be used as a basis for discrimination, but will be judged on its relevance to the position you are seeking. Wolfe It Down, Inc., a franchisee of XXXXXXXXXXX, is an equal opportunity employer.

Please complete the entire application to ensure processing.

PERSONAL INFORMATION (Please print)

Date: 10 / 1 / 12

Name (Last)	First	Middle	Do you have a Social Security Number?
EMPLOYEE	POTENTIAL	NEW	X Yes ____ No

Are you less than 18 years of age? X Yes ____ No   (We are required to comply with federal and state laws concerning the employment of minors.)

Present Address	City	State	ZIP Code
12345 6th St.	Anytown	WA	00000

Phone Number:	Email Address:	How were you referred to this company?
425-XXX-XXXX	me@xxxxxx.com	by your website

EMPLOYMENT DESIRED

(Please keep in mind that the availability of hours may vary.)

Position: Crew Member   Date You Can Start: ASAP

	Mon 8am-8pm	Tue 8am-8pm	Wed 8am-8pm	Thu 8am-8pm	Fri 8am-9pm	Sat 8am-9pm	Sun 8am-8pm
We are open seven days a week:							
What hours would you be available to work for each day of the week?	3:30-8	3:30-8	X	3:30-8	X	any	any

Are you able to work overtime? ____ Yes X No

Have you worked for our company before? no   If Yes: where and when? _____

LEGAL

(All new hires will be required to provide proof of eligibility to work in the U.S.)

Are you legally eligible to work in the U.S.? X Yes ____ No

Have you been convicted of a crime in the last seven years or are currently under felony indictment? ____ Yes X No
If Yes, list convictions or indictments that are a matter of public record (arrests are not convictions). This will not necessarily disqualify you for employment.

Convictions/ Indictments: _____

Was your employment ever terminated by any of your previous employers? ____ Yes ____ No X N/A

If Yes, please give the name of the company or companies, and describe the reason(s) why your employment was terminated: _____

U.S. MILITARY SERVICE

	Branch of Service	Technical Specialization	Rank Attained
N/A			

EDUCATION

	Name and Location of School	Did you graduate?	Last Year Completed	Degree/ Area of Study
High School	Anytown H.S., Anytown, WA	Y (N)	1 (2) 3 4	general; college prep
College	N/A	Y N	1 2 3 4	
Trade School	N/A	Y N	1 2 3 4	
Other	N/A	Y N	1 2 3 4	

GENERAL INFORMATION

List any skills, training, hobbies, classes, subjects of special interest, etc.

golf, singing, play guitar, taking German class, on track team

What special tools or equipment can you operate?	Can you operate a computer? X Yes ____ No
N/A	If Yes, what programs? Word, Excel, Publisher

FORMER EMPLOYERS

List your last three employers, starting with the most recent one first.
Please complete this section even if you attach a resume.

Date (M/D/Y)	Name and Address of Employer	Wages	Position(s) Held
From: To:	I have no former employers. This would be my first job.	Starting:_____ Ending:_____ If hourly, average number of hours per week: _____	
What was your reason for leaving: _____			

Date (M/D/Y)	Name and Address of Employer	Wages	Position(s) Held
From: To:	N/A	Starting:_____ Ending:_____ If hourly, average number of hours per week: _____	
What was your reason for leaving: _____			

Date (M/D/Y)	Name and Address of Employer	Wages	Position(s) Held
From: To:	N/A	Starting:_____ Ending:_____ If hourly, average number of hours per week: _____	
What was your reason for leaving: _____			

PLEASE READ CAREFULLY

Signature _Potential Employee_ Date _10-1-12_

WOLFE IT DOWN, INC.
a Franchisee of XXXXXXXXXXXXXXXXX
XXXX W. Union Hills Drive, Suite 101
XXXXXXX, XX XXXXX

WE ARE AN EQUAL OPPORTUNITY EMPLOYER
COMMITTED TO HIRING A DIVERSE WORKFORCE.

23

Lesson Plan for Day 4: "Survive and Advance"

Agenda:
- Album Two: Pages 33-43

Time Commitment:
- One full class period

Details:
You will ask for and answer questions from the previous class's homework assignment, then hand out Quiz 2. After your students turn in the completed quizzes, discuss each question and give them the answers if time allows.

Goals:
- Have students gain an awareness and understanding of the various steps in the weeding-out process.
- Have students reflect on their own current style of communication, and how that might help or hurt their chances of finding a job.

Review Prior to Quiz 2:
Ask for questions, and prompt the discussion with these:

- Out in the working world, in the world of business, which do you think is the more widely used form of communication: texting or emailing? (*Emailing is by far the dominant of the two. Texting is for personal communication which, by the way, you don't want to do a lot of while at work. Or school.*)
- Why is it important to check your email at least once a day when you are out there applying for jobs? (*Many potential employers will be contacting you via email, not texting.*)
- If you happen to get an email from a potential employer, how quickly are you expected to respond? (*Within a day or two at the latest.*)
- If you don't respond quickly, what might that employer think about you? (*You are no longer interested; you didn't like the questions they were asking you; you didn't think they would like your answers to those questions.*)
- What does it mean when a company says they have a "zero-tolerance" policy? (*One strike and you are out when it comes to drug and alcohol use while on the job; and also theft. Many companies also have very little tolerance for behaviors such as dishonesty, insubordination, laziness and tardiness.*)
- If you have a large tattoo of a skull and crossbones on your forearm, how will that affect your ability to get a job? (*Most companies do not allow visible/objectionable tattoos while at work, so it could hurt your chances greatly.*)
- If a company calls you on the phone, what would be some big turn-offs that you want to avoid? (*Sounding un-energetic, disrespectful, cocky, cool, unmotivated.*)
- What is an employer really looking for when they call you on the phone? (*They are checking your verbal communication skills; they want to hear if you sound energetic, enthusiastic, polite, respectful and self-confident.*)
- If a company were to call you and get your voicemail <u>right now</u>, what does your voicemail message sound like? (*You might ask for volunteers to put their voicemail messages on speaker-phone so the class can hear it and evaluate it.*)
- How quickly will someone judge you during a phone interview? (*In the first minute or two.*)

Hand Out Quiz 2: Questions from Album Two
Collect quizzes for review/grading. Review answers if time allows.

Homework Assignment:

"Read pages 45-75 and be prepared to discuss the information in the next class. It sounds like a lot of reading, but you can actually read this entire book in two hours or less."

Tell your students that they have survived the weeding-out process, and now they have been selected to come in for a face-to-face interview. How they look, how they act, how they speak, and how well they answer the interview questions will be critical in their quest to land the job. The best way to prepare for a face-to-face interview is to know what to expect, and to practice ahead of time. This section of the book will prepare you for this final important step in the process.

Evaluation:

When this class meets again, you will hand out a quiz after you have reviewed and discussed the homework material.

The Part-Timer Primer ™   NAME_____

Quiz 2

"Survive and Advance"

Circle the <u>one</u> answer you think is correct for each question. For questions that require you to write in the answer, please write neatly and clearly; unreadable answers will be considered incorrect.

1. During the job interview process, the purpose of a business owner sending you a screening email is to:

    a) reduce the chances of talking to someone who is not going to be a good fit for the company.

    b) identify and eliminate weak candidates.

    c) add you to their list of contacts.

    d) check to see if your email is working.

    e) both a) and b).

2. If a business has a policy of "zero tolerance" regarding an issue, then it means:

    a) you can mess up once and get a second chance.

    b) the rules apply to everyone else, but not you.

    c) mistakes happen and bosses understand that.

    d) if you mess up one time, then you will be fired; no discussion, no second chance-- you are gone.

3. Visible tattoos and piercings can prevent you from getting a job because:

    a) business owners want their employees to project a clean-cut, professional image to their customers.

    b) some business owners don't want their employees to be cooler than they are.

    c) customers are going to perceive a business either positively or negatively in large part to how the employees look.

    d) both a) and c).

4. If an employer sends you a screening email, you are expected to respond:

    a) whenever you get around to it.

    b) within one week because they know that these days people text more than they check their email.

    c) the same day, or the next day at the latest.

    d) by calling them back or stopping in to see them.

5. Why are your speaking skills so important during a phone call with a potential employer?

_____

_____

6. During a phone interview, you want to leave the impression that:

    a) you are cool, cocky and popular.

    b) you are self-confident without being cocky.

    c) you are polite, courteous and respectful.

    d) both a) and c).

    e) both b) and c).

7. In the business world, people use the word "like" all the time when speaking to customers and suppliers because that's how most business people talk.

    True   False

8. The proper way to address a potential employer is by using words such as:

    a) hello, sir.

    b) buddy.

    c) hey man.

    d) yes, ma'am.

    e) both a) and d).

    f) both b) and c).

9. Many employers will decide if they think you have potential or not in the first minute or two of a phone conversation.

True   False

10. Your voice mail message will have no influence on a potential employer. It's your private greeting to your friends. It does not make any difference.

True   False

The Part-Timer Primer ™
Quiz 2
"Survive and Advance"

Answer Guide and Page References

Question 1: During the job interview process, the purpose of a business owner sending you a screening email is to:

   a) reduce the chances of talking to someone who is not going to be a good fit for the company.

   b) identify and eliminate weak candidates.

   c) add you to their list of contacts.

   d) check to see if your email is working.

   e) both a) and b).

Answer: e) both a) and b).

Discussion (page 34): The job app and survey profile are good starting points in the weeding-out process, but they don't provide the employer with enough information to further narrow the list of job candidates. Remember that employers want to streamline the process and talk to only a few people; they don't have time to meet with everyone. The email screen will eliminate a huge number of applicants. It will often reduce the pile to the five or six people who will receive phone calls.

Question 2: If a business has a policy of "zero tolerance" regarding an issue, then it means:

   a) you can mess up once and get a second chance.

   b) the rules apply to everyone else, but not you.

   c) mistakes happen and bosses understand that.

   d) if you mess up one time, then you will be fired; no discussion, no second chance-- you are gone.

Answer: d) if you mess up one time, then you will be fired; no discussion, no second chance-- you are gone.

Discussion (page 34): This might seem pretty harsh at first glance, especially when dealing with young adults who have no work experience. After all, nobody is perfect, right? We all make mistakes. But zero-tolerance issues don't deal with small procedural errors or mistakes that happen while learning a new skill. We're talking about bigger issues such as theft, dishonesty, drug use-- these are serious problems that relate to someone's integrity and moral character. With respect to drug or alcohol use, it's illegal activity that can lead to serious errors in judgment. It's not just the user who is at risk; customers, co-workers, even the entire business entity can be jeopardized.

Imagine what would happen if a foodhandler under the influence of drugs or alcohol forgets to follow safe foodhandling guidelines, and a customer suffers a severe case of food poisoning which leads to death. Now a zero-tolerance policy doesn't seem so harsh after all. There are certain risks a business simply cannot afford to take.

Question 3: Visible tattoos and piercings can prevent you from getting a job at many companies because:

 a) business owners want their employees to project a clean-cut, professional image to their customers.

 b) some business owners don't want their employees to be cooler than they are.

 c) customers are going to perceive a business either positively or negatively in large part to how the employees look.

 d) both a) and c).

Answer: d) both a) and c).

Discussion (page 36): Tattoos and piercings are common outlets for personal expression these days, and it's tough to discuss this issue without sounding preachy or judgmental. There is no hard and fast rule, and there is plenty of gray area. Is it really a big deal if someone has a small tattoo of a rose on their ankle? If they have two sets of earrings in each ear? If there's a tiny diamond on their nostril? OK, what about a skull and crossbones on someone's forearm? Images of fierce-looking animals? Barbed wire? Colorful designs that cover someone's entire right arm from wrist to shoulder? Where do you draw the line?

The thing to keep in mind is that your method of personal expression may not fit in with the philosophy of many companies. From a business perspective, you might be severely limiting your job opportunities. You have to start thinking about this issue in terms of finding a balance between how you want to express yourself and what you want to do for a job or a career. As a teen with no work experience, you may not have any idea what kind of work you want to do to make a living as an adult. So you might want to keep as many options open as possible at this stage of your life.

Question 4: If an employer sends you a screening email, you are expected to respond:

a) whenever you get around to it.

b) within one week because they know that these days people text more than they check their email.

c) the same day, or the next day at the latest.

d) by calling them back or stopping in to see them.

Answer: c) <u>the same day, or the next day at the latest.</u>

Discussion (page 39): As a business owner, I am surprised at the number of times a job applicant with a solid job app and good survey profile will not respond to my email until a week to 10 days later. By the time they respond and I see that they have no issues with my policies, I've already moved on to other candidates and may have even hired someone else. It seems that texting has overtaken emailing as the preferred method of communication among young adults. But in the business world, emailing is still a dominant form of communication and an important tool for recruiting and hiring. Someone who is looking for a job must regularly check their email or risk losing out on an opportunity.

Question 5: Why are your speaking skills so important during a phone call with a potential employer?

Answer: <u>Responses should relate to leaving a good first impression.</u>

Discussion (page 40): The purpose of the initial phone call is to check your verbal communication skills. How you speak will leave a certain impression about you. Like it or not, people will judge you by how you speak. They'll quickly form opinions about your level of intelligence, education, maturity, energy, and your attitude about work-- all based on how you speak. Employers want to hear how you sound, because that's how you will sound in front of their customers. Will you leave a positive impression with their customers when you speak to them? Do you sound like you would be an enthusiastic, hard-working employee? Or a deadbeat?

Question 6: During a phone interview, you want to leave the impression that:

a) you are cool, cocky and popular.

b) you are self-confident without being cocky.

c) you are polite, courteous and respectful.

d) both a) and c).

e) both b) and c).

Answer: e) <u>both b) and c).</u>

Discussion (page 41): Respect is a big deal to business owners and managers. They've "done their time" and have "paid their dues" to get where they are. The sacrifices they've made, the risks they've taken, and the challenges they've overcome will never be understood or appreciated by someone who has never even had a job before. Nevertheless, they expect to be spoken to with a measure of respect and courtesy. They're not going to have much tolerance for an inexperienced "kid" who comes across as a know-it-all or as someone who is entitled to the job.

Question 7: In the business world, it's OK to use the word "like" all the time when speaking to customers and suppliers because that's how most business people talk.

   True   False

Answer: <u>False</u>

Discussion (page 41): When adults hear a young person overusing the word "like" in a conversation, it can be either funny or irritating depending on the situation. To an employer it's definitely a turn-off. You don't want to leave the impression that you haven't yet learned how to adequately explain your thought or express your comment in a complete, intelligent sentence. The word "like" is a short-cut: people use it in place of more proper grammar. Look at these examples; the word or phrase in parentheses is a more accepted way of speaking in the business world:

"So I was <u>like</u> (thinking to myself), wow, what was that all about?"

" And then <u>it was like</u> (I realized) I have to get this done before the deadline."

"I knew I was going to be <u>like</u> (really) late for work so I was <u>like</u> (wondering) what should I do now?"

"It's <u>like</u> (as if) nobody is listening to me."

"And then I <u>was like</u> (said), I'm so sorry for the long wait; how may I help you?"

"After that I was <u>like</u> (feeling) really happy."

Question 8: The proper way to address a potential employer is with words such as:

   a) hello, sir.

   b) buddy.

   c) hey man.

   d) yes, ma'am.

   e) both a) and d).

   f) both b) and c).

Answer: e) both a) and d).

Discussion (page 41): This goes back to the issue of respect in Question 6. Imagine a new soldier being introduced to a commanding officer and saying, "How's it going, buddy?" How well do you think that would go over?

In so many areas of life there is a rank and an order to interpersonal relationships. You have the parent/child relationship; the teacher/student relationship; the boss/employee relationship; the coach/player relationship; the officer/enlisted person relationship; and other superior/subordinate relationships. In all of these, there is a certain "code of conduct" in which respect plays a big role. If you violate that code, intentionally or unintentionally, there can be consequences.

In this example, trying to become an instant "buddy" or "friend" with a potential employer is going to backfire on you. That just shows them that you do not yet understand or respect the authority of their position or your role in the relationship.

Question 9: Many employers will decide if they think you have potential or not in the first minute or two of a phone conversation.

True   False

Answer: True

Discussion (page 42): The old saying still rings true: "You never get a second chance to make a first impression." Even though they've never met you, employers are painting a mental picture of you as they are speaking with you over the phone. They might be comparing you to other employees they have-- or had. They're listening to your tone of voice, the words and phrases you use, and your energy level. Do you sound like a bright, mature, enthusiastic person who "gets" the whole courtesy and respect thing? Or not? It's amazing how quickly we all form opinions. And once someone's mind is made up about something or someone, it's almost impossible to change it.

Question 10: Your voice mail message will have no influence on a potential employer. It's your private greeting to your friends. It does not make any difference.

True   False

Answer: False

Discussion (Page 43): When it's time for you to start looking for a job, you have to think about things like this. It's not just your friends who will be calling you anymore. It could be a potential employer. What are they going to hear, and what impression is that going to leave with them? If you're not leaving the impression that you are a responsible young adult, then you are hurting your chances of landing that first job.

Lesson Plan for Day 5: "Finally Face-to-Face"

Agenda:
- Album Three: Pages 45-75

Time Commitment:
- One full class period

Details:
You will ask for and answer any questions from the previous class's homework assignment, then hand out Quiz 3. After your students turn in the completed quizzes, discuss each question and give them the answers if time allows.

Goals:
- Let students know what to anticipate and how to prepare for a face-to-face job interview.

Review Prior to Quiz 3:
Ask for questions, and prompt the discussion with these:

- Let's say you have a job interview at 4pm. It's now 3:45pm; you are stuck in traffic and you might or might not make it to the interview on time. What should you do? (*Call the interviewer and apologize that you are on your way but you might be a few minutes late because of bad traffic. Ask if this is still OK or if the interviewer would like to reschedule.*)
- Describe how you should be dressed and groomed for a job interview. (*Classy-casual; clean; not wrinkled and messy; no jeans; no flip-flops; no gum chewing; guys clean-shaven and minimal cologne; girls neatly dressed; no overkill on the jewelry and perfumes.*)
- Even without you saying a word, you are still sending out messages whether you realize it or not. What are these forms of non-verbal communication called? (*Body language.*)
- Give me some examples of non-verbal forms of communication. (*A handshake; eye contact; nervous fidgeting; slouching.*)
- Even if you are not feeling very self-confident going into a job interview, is it possible to fake your way through it? (*Yes; it happens all the time. A firm handshake, a smile, good eye contact, and a tone of voice that sounds assertive will get you through it. You might surprise yourself after you've done it.*)
- What's the best way to prepare for a job interview? (*Anticipate what is going to happen, and practice!*)
- What do you think I mean when I say, "Repetition is the mother of skill?" (*The more you practice, the better you'll get.*)

Hand Out Quiz 3: Questions from Album Three
Collect quizzes for review/grading. Review answers if time allows.

Homework Assignment:
"Study and practice answering the 20 questions (21 actually) listed in the book that someone might ask you during a job interview." Encourage them to practice out loud and in front of a mirror. They may even want to get together and practice with each other. In your next class, you as the instructor are going to play the role of the job interviewer. You will be calling on individual students to answer out loud the question you ask each of them. This will be a good "role playing" experience for your students.

Evaluation:
Next class you will be evaluating your students by how well they are prepared to answer your "21 Questions." You will be listening for how well they practiced their answers. Did they stumble over their words? How was their tone of voice? What did their body language tell you?

The Part-Timer Primer ™   NAME_____

Quiz 3

"Finally Face-to-Face"

Circle the <u>one</u> answer you think is correct for each question. For questions that require you to write in the answer, please write neatly and clearly; unreadable answers will be considered incorrect.

1. If you know you'll be running late for an interview, the thing to do is:

  a) don't do anything; just get there as soon as you can.

  b) come up with a good excuse and make sure they know it wasn't your fault.

  c) call at least 15 minutes before you are supposed to be there, and apologize that you are running a little late.

  d) when you get there, just act like you are on time.

2. It's never too early to show up for an interview. Early is always good.

          True   False

3. Most businesses have grooming standards that must be followed, so it's best to assume that:

  a) those same standards apply to a job interview.

  b) you can wear anything you want to a job interview because you don't work there yet.

  c) young men should wear a suit and tie just to be safe, and young women should always wear a nice dress.

4. Non-verbal forms of communication, known as "body language," would include:

  a) your handshake.

  b) eye contact.

  c) being fidgety.

  d) facial expressions.

  e) all of the above.

5. Of the 20 interview questions listed in the book, how many of them should you be prepared to answer?

    a) at least half of them.

    b) all of them.

    c) you can't really prepare because you have no idea which questions will be asked of you.

    d) only the first seven questions, because nobody asks more than seven.

6. Write a brief and polite response to this request: "Tell me about yourself."

_____

_____

_____

_____

7. During a job interview, you have to answer every question that the interviewer asks you.

    True   False

8. When you are practicing your answers to the "20 questions" you should:

    a) say them out loud.

    b) rehearse them silently in your head so you don't disturb anybody.

    c) practice in front of a mirror.

    d) both a) and c).

9. If you are the one who is asking some intelligent questions during the interview, that will make you look like:

    a) you are trying to take control of the interview.

    b) you are unprepared.

    c) you are interested in the company and the job.

10. For many entry-level positions, the face-to-face interview is one of the final steps and is mostly a "chemistry check" with the employer and the crew.

True   False

11. After the interview, you should go home and:

    a) wait for the phone to ring.

    b) send a follow-up email to the interviewer, thanking them for their time.

    c) call to see if you got the job.

    d) take a nap.

12. If you don't get the job, you'll have to accept the fact that you may never learn the real reason why you were not chosen.

    True   False

13. List at least three personal qualities or values that employers look for in a potential new employee:

_____

_____

_____

_____

The Part-Timer Primer ™
Quiz 3
"Finally Face-to-Face"

Answer Guide and Page References

Question 1: If you know you'll be running late for an interview, the thing to do is:

   a) don't do anything; just get there as soon as you can.

   b) come up with a really good excuse and make sure they know it wasn't your fault.

   c) call at least 15 minutes before you are supposed to be there, and apologize that you are running a little late.

   d) when you get there, just act like you are on time.

Answer: c) <u>call at least 15 minutes before you are supposed to be there, and apologize that you are running a little late.</u>

Discussion (page 45): Nobody is on time all the time. But being late for a job interview is not a good thing. Some delays are unavoidable (such as getting a flat tire on the way), but most delays can be averted simply by giving yourself more time to get there. Many of the excuses will not go over well with the business owner or manager. You got stuck in traffic? You should have given yourself more time. You got lost, or it took you longer to get there than you thought it would take? You should have spent more time studying where the location was. Your ride was late picking you up? It doesn't sound like you have reliable transportation.

Whatever the reason, you need to call and let the interviewer know that you are very sorry to be running a few minutes late. By calling ahead of time, you are showing consideration and respect. This phone call could very well save the day for you.

If you are someone who is habitually late for <u>everything</u>, you need to fix that. Quickly. Or else you are going to have a tough road ahead of you. Being late all the time sends off a signal to others that you are either very disorganized-- or that you just don't care. Neither of those are labels you want to have attached to your name.

Question 2: It's never too early to show up for an interview. Early is always good.

   True   False

Answer: <u>False</u>

Discussion (page 46): Being <u>too early</u> is not good. You'll probably interrupt the interviewer who'll be in the middle of some other task. They scheduled you at a certain time for a reason; respect their time and show them you can follow instructions. Don't be too early.

I've heard this argument before: "If I give myself extra time to get there and nothing happens, then I'll be there really early. I don't want to just sit around and waste my time; I might as well go in now."

But it's not about <u>your</u> time; it's about the interviewer's time. If you happen to be very early, go kill some time somewhere close by. Run a quick errand, do some studying, make some phone calls you've been meaning to make. Respect the interviewer's time, and they will respect you.

Question 3: Most businesses have grooming standards that must be followed, so it's best to assume that:

   a) those same standards apply to a job interview.

   b) you can wear anything you want to a job interview because you don't work there yet.

   c) young men should wear a suit and tie just to be safe, and young women should always wear a nice dress.

Answer: a) <u>those same standards apply to a job interview</u>.

Discussion (page 48): You might as well look the part from the start. If you're not dressed appropriately, it sends the wrong message about you-- especially if you are <u>underdressed</u>. If you show up in flip-flops and a tank top, that's way too casual. It tells the interviewer that this opportunity is not very important to you. And it comes off as a sign of disrespect.

"You couldn't even take the time to dress in something better than that? You think it's OK to wear whatever you feel like wearing? You don't think my business is worthy of more than that? Sorry, but you don't get it."

I'd much rather see someone overdressed than underdressed. Being overdressed tells me that this opportunity is very important to them, and that they took some time to stop and think about what they should wear.

Question 4: Non-verbal forms of communication, known as "body language," would include:

    a) your handshake.

    b) eye contact.

    c) being fidgety.

    d) facial expressions.

    e) all of the above.

Answer: e) <u>all of the above.</u>

Discussion (page 52): Have you ever looked into someone's eyes to try and figure out if they are lying to you? If you have, then you were studying their body language. If you shook someone's hand and their handshake felt soft and limp, what impression did that leave with you? Have your parents or teachers ever caught you in a lie? How do you think they figured it out?

Many experts on human behavior believe that your body language communicates much more than the words you use. "The body doesn't lie" is an expression I've heard before. It's very hard to control your own body language; most of the time you are not even aware of what signals you are giving off. That's why non-verbal forms of communication are considered more accurate indicators of the real message being sent.

Question 5: Of the 20 interview questions listed in the book, how many of them should you be prepared to answer?

    a) at least half of them.

    b) all of them.

    c) you can't really prepare because you have no idea which questions will be asked of you.

    d) only the first seven questions, because nobody asks more than seven.

Answer: b) <u>all of them.</u>

Discussion (page 54): There's no way to predict with 100% accuracy which questions someone will ask you. But no matter what the questions are, it's important for you to understand that business owners and managers are all trying to determine the same things about you: would you be reliable, dependable, hard-working, trustworthy? If you are prepared to answer these 20 questions, and you understand <u>why</u> they are asking you these questions, then you'll be in a much better position to confidently answer any other question someone else might ask you.

Question 6: Write a brief and polite response to this request: "Tell me about yourself."

Answer: Answers will vary based on each individual student.

Discussion (page 60): This is not difficult to answer if you are prepared for it. Your answer should include a few different "talking points" about you that the interviewer can expand on.

Question 7: During a job interview, you have to answer every question that the interviewer asks you.

    True   False

Answer: False

Discussion (page 62): The questions you would not be required to answer are ones that involve issues of potential discrimination. Questions about your ethnicity or religious beliefs are examples of questions that you most likely would not have to answer. In this Information Age that we live in, most owners and managers who've been around a while are quite familiar with interview questions that can and cannot be asked. It's the people newer to supervisory positions who sometimes slip up and ask things they shouldn't.

If I were a 16-year old looking for my first job, I would probably answer every question and then, after the interview was over, reflect on whether any of the questions were inappropriate and if I would feel comfortable working for the person who asked them. A question such as, "how old are you?" seems pretty harmless compared to others such as, "do you have a boyfriend?" or "are you Asian or Mexican?"

Nothing says you have to accept the job if you felt the interviewer was asking personal questions that made you uncomfortable. I would pass on that opportunity and keep looking.

Question 8: When you are practicing your answers to the "20 questions" you should:

    a) say them out loud.

    b) rehearse them silently in your head so you don't disturb anybody.

    c) practice in front of a mirror.

    d) both a) and c).

 Answer: d) both a) and c).

Discussion (page 65): You will be amazed at how much better and more confident you will be if you practice out loud in front of a mirror. What you are saying to yourself "silently" in your head is not what is going to come out of your mouth smoothly and effortlessly.

Answering interview questions is a bit like public speaking. To get really good at it, like anything else, you have to practice. If you want to practice shooting free throws, you can't just stand there and think about it-- you have to go through the mechanics and the motions of actually directing the basketball to the hoop. If you're going to practice the skill of speaking, you have to speak. Out loud. Doing it in front of a mirror allows you to check your facial expressions while you are speaking. You want to make sure that you appear calm and confident-- even if you're not.

Question 9: If you are the one who is asking some intelligent questions during the interview, that will make you look like:

   a) you are trying to take control of the interview.

   b) you are unprepared.

   c) you are interested in the company and the job.

Answer: c) <u>you are interested in the company and the job.</u>

Discussion (page 66): The key point here is to ask some <u>intelligent</u> questions. You might have heard the phrase, "there's no such thing as a dumb question." Oh yes there is. If you walk into an interview at a McDonald's hamburger restaurant and ask, "what kind of business is this?" then you obviously have not done any homework beforehand. Here are some better questions to ask:

"What are your busiest days and times?"

"What is the most popular item on the menu?"

"What is the most difficult thing for a brand new person to learn?"

"What are the biggest mistakes a new person makes?"

"If I were hired and did a good job, what would it take to get promoted?"

You should be prepared to ask at least a couple of questions to show that you are interested in the company and the job. Of course the interviewer already knows you are curious about how much you would get paid and how many hours you would get, so you don't want to ask those until after you have been offered the job.

Question 10: For many entry-level positions, the face-to-face interview is one of the final steps and is mostly a "chemistry check" with the employer and the crew.

   True   False

Answer: <u>True</u>

Discussion (Page 68): If you get this far in the hiring process, you are one of the finalists. At this point, the owner or hiring manager is going to be watching for any clues that would suggest you might not be a good fit. They'll be watching your body language and listening to your tone of voice to see if you appear as calm, confident and excited about the opportunity as you sounded on the phone or described in your email response. They'll be watching their own employees to see how they are reacting to your presence there. If you talk to some of the employees, they will give their feedback to the boss after you have left.

Of course you will be on your best behavior and they know that. But does it seem natural and comfortable for you to be that way? Or does it seem fake and forced? This is all part of the "chemistry check."

Question 11: After the interview, you should go home and:

  a) wait for the phone to ring.

  b) send a follow-up email to the interviewer, thanking them for their time.

  c) call to see if you got the job.

  d) take a nap.

Answer: b) <u>send a follow-up email to the interviewer, thanking them for their time.</u>

Discussion (Page 70): If you did not get the interviewer's email address during your particular hiring process, be sure to ask for it at the end of the interview: "May I follow up with you via email?" Very few first-time job hunters take this important step in following up. It truly does leave a positive impression, and it could be the tie-breaker that gets you the job.

Hint: if you ask for their email address and you get a response such as, "Oh that's OK, I've got your email and phone number so I'll be in touch," that's not a good sign. You're getting the "don't call us, we'll call you" routine, which means the interview did not go well. Bummer. Back to the drawing board to figure out what went wrong.

Question 12: If you don't get the job, you'll have to accept the fact that you may never learn the real reason why you were not chosen.

  True   False

Answer: <u>True</u>

Discussion (Page 73): It's a tough lesson to learn for many of us: life isn't always fair. And so many decisions are made for emotional or irrational reasons, which means they don't make logical sense at all. But that's the way it is; it's human nature. Have you ever been in a situation yourself where you needed to say no to somebody but you didn't really want to tell them the real reason why? Maybe it was because you didn't want to hurt their feelings?

If you don't get the job, one of the hardest things for anybody to do is to take a good, honest look at yourself and see if you can figure out why. Did you make a mistake somewhere in something you said or did? Is there something physically about you that might be holding you back? Was your body language sending the wrong message? Were you prepared enough to answer the questions? Self-analysis is an extremely difficult-- and sometimes unpleasant task.

Question 13: List at least three personal qualities or values that employers look for in a potential new employee:

Answer: <u>Any of the following:</u>

Reliable	**Dependable**	**Mature**
Self-disciplined	**Strong work ethic**	**Positive attitude**
Pleasant personality	**Team Player**	**Respectful**
Courteous	**Coachable**	**Honest**
Trustworthy		

Discussion (Page 75): The more of these qualities you can demonstrate, the better your chances will be to land a job. If you're a good, honest, hard-working person, does that guarantee that you'll get the job? No. Remember that not all decisions make logical sense. But being a good, honest, hard-working person will greatly improve your chances.

Lesson Plan for Day 6: "Role Playing"

Agenda:
- Interview Questions: in-class role playing

Time Commitment:
- One full class period

Details:
You, the instructor, will play the role of the interviewer. You could approach this session a couple of different ways. In one scenario, each of your students will be "interviewed" for an entry-level job, and you will ask a question or two of each student. Or, if you know some of your students would be completely traumatized by this, you could select a couple of your more confident students and ask them most of the 21 questions listed in the book. You might also throw in a couple of unexpected questions and see how they respond.

Goals:
- Give your students the opportunity to practice their interviewing skills.
- Give your students the real-world experience of a job interview in the somewhat protected environment of your classroom.
- Reinforce the fact that practicing out loud will make someone more comfortable and confident in an interview situation.

Evaluation:
As you ask the questions, you will be evaluating your students by how well they are prepared to answer them. You will be listening for how well they practiced their answers. Did they stumble over their words? How was their tone of voice? What did their body language tell you?

Role-Playing Questions to Ask Your Students

1. How is school going for you these days? I'm going to listen carefully to your answer to find out if you are applying yourself and trying your best. I'll also be listening to see if you enjoy school or not. I'd rather hire someone who has a healthy, positive attitude toward learning. You don't necessarily have to have excellent grades to get a job, but you do have to convince me you're trying your hardest.

2. What are your favorite classes/subjects and why? I want to know what interests you, and in what areas your skills might be. Everyone has their own unique set of skills, strengths and weaknesses. I'm trying to find yours.

3. If I were to ask your teachers about you, how do you think they would describe you? Teachers are a great resource of information. They'll tell me if you are a problem student or not. Chances are good that a problem student will be a problem employee. That's a problem I want to avoid.

4. How often are you late for class? You're probably going to answer "Never" but I'm letting you know that punctuality is important. I tell my new employees early on, "One of the fastest ways to lose your job is to be late for work." You have to be reliable all the time, every day.

5. How often do you miss school because of illness or other reasons? Everyone gets sick once or twice a year. But once or twice a month? That's a problem. If you miss a lot of school, you'll probably miss a lot of work.

6. Do you participate in lots of after-school activities? Be up front about your extracurricular activities and how much time you are going to need off, what days, hours etc. Don't hide those things in order to get the job. If I find out after the fact, at best I'll be irritated. At worst I might re-consider my decision and send you packing.

7. What other hobbies or interests do you have? I'm probing to see if you are a well-rounded person. I want employees who are engaged in the process of life. Do you view your life as drudgery? Or do you view it as an adventure with new things to discover all the time? I'm also looking for clues as to whether you are a "loner" or someone who likes to have other people around them. Do you participate in team sports or other group activities? Do you practice good sportsmanship? At a job you will be working closely with other crew members. How well I think you would work with my other employees is a determining factor.

8. Can you give me any examples that would demonstrate how you are a dependable person? Since you have no work history, I need something else to go by. Maybe you walk your dog every day right after school. Or you babysit every Friday night for your neighbors. Or you help your mom with chores every Saturday morning. I'm looking for evidence that shows you might be a reliable employee if I hire you.

9. What sort of volunteer work have you participated in? Volunteer work says something about your character; that you are able to look beyond your own personal needs; that it's not always about you or about money. It's unusual to find young people with volunteer experience. But when I do, it's a plus.

10. Many successful people believe that we learn more from our mistakes than from our successes. Can you give me an example of a mistake you made, and what you learned from it? Nobody likes to admit that they messed up. We all do. We might be good, but we're not perfect. If you can admit that you screwed up, and you can explain what you learned from it, that's a sign of maturity:

11. What do you feel is your greatest strength? If you already know this about yourself, you're way ahead of where I was at your age. I'm looking for an asset than will help my business. Are you good at math? I could put you in charge of the cash register. Are you the captain of a sports team? Editor of the school paper? Class president? You're showing some leadership skills; maybe I could groom you into a more supervisory role later on.

12. What is something about yourself that you need to improve on? Another tough question, I know. Do you have trouble expressing yourself? Are you struggling in a particular class? Do you have a quick temper? Do you have a short attention span? If you're already mature enough to be analyzing your own weaknesses and working to improve them, that's a good sign.

13. Do you consider yourself to be an introvert (someone who is more comfortable being alone with their own thoughts and feelings) or an extrovert (someone who is more outgoing and sociable)? There is no right or wrong answer here. Introverts tend to be better at listening (which is much easier to do when you're not talking). Introverts tend to think things through carefully, which leads to a better chance of making good decisions and fewer mistakes. Extroverts can be great at customer service positions because they enjoy the social interaction. There's a role in business for both types.

14. When you are faced with a math problem, do you always use a calculator to figure it out, or are you able to do some math in your head or on paper? Many jobs will take some math skills, and you won't have access to a calculator every time. A customer at the counter might hand you the wrong amount of money, and you have to figure out the correct amount of change quickly because there's a long line of customers waiting ever more impatiently behind him. You might be counting SKU's (stock keeping units) on the back shelves of a warehouse; you only have 13 in stock and you should be stocked at 45. How many do you need to order? You need to make a double batch of pizza dough today; the recipe says a single batch takes 10.75 pounds of water. How much do you need for a double batch? (See, you really <u>do</u> need to learn this stuff!)

15. If you were walking out of a store and realized that the cashier forgot to charge you for one of the items you bought, what would you do? Would you go back and pay for the item? Would you keep walking out of the store, feeling like you got a good deal? Your response will tell me something about your honesty and integrity.

16. Some people learn a new skill by reading about it; some learn by observing someone else doing it; others learn by listening to someone explain how to do it. How do you think you like to learn new things? If you haven't thought about this before, then my question will get you thinking. Based on how you like to learn, I might start your training with some online videos. Or I might have you shadow one of my supervisors so you can watch how they do it. Or I could have you read our employee manual first.

17. Sometimes you'll see the coach of a team yelling at his players during a game. It doesn't mean that he doesn't like his players. He's trying to correct something they're not doing properly, and get them to perform at their best all the time. If a boss is yelling at you, how do you think you would handle that? Getting yelled at is stressful. In a work situation, some people will be embarrassed or offended if they are corrected in front of co-workers. Some will have a "know it all" attitude and will stubbornly refuse to admit they're not doing it right. Others will whine about it to their co-workers. Sometimes, they'll get very upset and quit.

In a brand new job, I expect new employees to be open to corrective comments without getting upset. It's hard to keep your cool under pressure, I know. I'm trying to find out if you are open to suggestions, receptive to a better way of performing a task, responsive in a positive way, even if you get "pushed" to improve your performance.

One of the many signs I have hanging in my store is this one: "Find out what the boss doesn't like, and don't do that." I'm only half-joking when I say that. I admit to getting a bit irritated when an employee continually ignores my advice. (On rare occasion I'll have to put my foot down and say, "I'm sorry but this is not a request; I need you to do it this way.")

18. Let's say you are making pizzas at a pizza restaurant, and a customer accuses you of putting the wrong toppings on their pizza. You're almost certain that you made it correctly. How would you handle that situation? Would you argue with the customer and tell them they are wrong? Would you apologize for the misunderstanding? Would you go get a supervisor to handle the situation? Would you make them a free pizza and not tell the supervisor? I'm looking to see how you would analyze a problem and make a decision.

19. Can you pass a drug test? You're going to say "Yes" for obvious reasons.

20. Can you pass a drug test *right now*? Sometimes I try to put the fear of God in you and see if you flinch. I'm going to watch your body language very closely as you answer. I consider myself to be a very good reader of non-verbal clues. If you look away; if you blush; if you hesitate…red flag. If you're going to lie to me on this answer, you better have a good poker face.

21. Tell me about yourself.

First of all, it's not even a question; it's a request. And it's a weak request at best.

The purpose of that request, supposedly, is to get you talking and see how comfortable you are in an obviously uncomfortable situation such as a job interview.

I don't think it's fair to request that of a young adult who is venturing out for the first time into the working world. I know of many adults, myself included, who've been working for decades and struggle mightily with that question.

It's a stall tactic: the interviewer is stalling because they aren't ready and don't know what questions they should be asking you.

What it really says about the interviewer is, "I'm unprepared. So I'm going to let you lead off to buy me some time."

It can also be a power play: the person making that request feels powerful in their position of authority, and they exert that power by making you squirm.

Shame on the interviewer.

Nevertheless, you should be prepared to answer that request with a brief, polite and pleasant response. Something like:

"I'm a senior at _____ High School; my favorite class is _____; I play the _____ in the school band; I have a dog named _____; I like to snowboard and I'm excited about the possibility of working here."

At least with an answer like that, you've bailed out the interviewer by offering up a couple of different directions they can take with their next questions.

Closing Comments

I hope we've demonstrated to you that there's a lot more to getting your first job than simply brushing your teeth, smiling and being polite. While those things are certainly important, there is a whole lot more to the process. And most of the weeding out happens long before you will ever get to the face-to-face interview. This weeding-out process doesn't happen exactly the same way in each company. But trust me, every company and every decision maker in that company has an evaluation process of some kind. They have to; there simply is not enough time in the day to thoroughly evaluate every single job application.

So…now that you are aware of this, and you know what to expect, and you know how to prepare for it, and you've practiced for it, you should feel a whole lot more confident in your chances of landing that first job.

Will knowing all of this and doing all of this guarantee that you'll get the job?

Nope. There are very few guarantees in life, unfortunately. And life is not always fair as you will find out along the way. But being prepared gives you a huge advantage over the majority of people who aren't. If you practice, prepare and be patient, chances are very good that it will happen for you.

What I can promise you is that there are plenty of employers out there who will be very pleasantly surprised, if not blown away, by you if you follow the guidance offered in this book. Once they hire you, they might even ask you if you have any other friends who are looking for work!

Best of luck, and let us know how it turns out!

Follow-up

If you follow the guidance offered in The Part-Timer Primer and you land that first job, please let us know! Go to our Facebook page and leave a comment about your experiences. We're at **www.facebook.com/parttimerprimer**. It would thrill us to no end and give us a great deal of satisfaction, knowing that we've helped you take that first leap into the working world!

Special Thanks

A big Thank You to brother Brian Doepke for his guidance in organizing the information in this Instructors Guide. He was an awesome teacher for many years before switching careers and becoming an awesome piano tuner.

www.ingramcontent.com/pod-product-compliance
Lightning Source LLC
Chambersburg PA
CBHW081232020426

42331CB00012B/3133